Cavalier King Charles Spaniel

Series "Fun Facts on Dogs for Kids"

Written by Michelle Hawkins

Cavalier King Charles Spaniel

Series "Fun Facts on Dogs for Kids"

By: Michelle Hawkins

Version 1.1 ~January 2021

Published by Michelle Hawkins at KDP

Cavalier King Charles Spaniel enjoys chasing squirrels.

Cavalier King Charles Spaniel is trainable with patience

**Cavalier King Charles Spaniel
can make a friend out of anyone.**

**Cavalier King Charles Spaniel
needs to have their teeth
brushed daily for fresh breathe.**

The life span for a Cavalier King Charles Spaniel is between twelve to fifteen years.

Before being known as Cavalier King Charles Spaniel, they were called small spaniels.

Cavalier King Charles Spaniel was named after King Charles II.

Cavalier King Charles Spaniel eats dog food, meat, and vegetables.

Cavalier King Charles Spaniel needs to be professional groomed at least every three months.

Cavalier King Charles Spaniel has a smooth and soft coat.

Cavalier King Charles Spaniel is suitable for a first-time dog owner.

Cavalier King Charles Spaniel is considered a family dog.

When training a Cavalier King Charles Spaniel, keep the training short.

Cavalier King Charles Spaniel breed was not recognized in the AKC till 1995.

Cavalier King Charles Spaniel would be a great companion for older adults.

Cavalier King Charles Spaniel must have a lot of human interaction.

Cavalier King Charles Spaniel enjoys chasing small animals.

Blenheim's spot on a Cavalier King Charles Spaniel is a red spot on their forehead.

Cavalier King Charles Spaniel is known for their beautiful face.

Cavalier King Charles Spaniel DNA is mixed with hunting dogs.

Cavalier King Charles Spaniel is in the top twenty breeds in America.

Cavalier King Charles Spaniel is very eager to please their owners.

Cavalier King Charles Spaniel can have separation anxiety.

Cavalier King Charles Spaniel does not need a lot of exercises.

Cavalier King Charles Spaniel will definitely drool on you.

There is no difference in size between the male and female Cavalier King Charles Spaniel.

Another name for the Cavalier King Charles Spaniel is the 'Comforter Spaniel.'

Cavalier King Charles Spaniel is known for its ears that are floppy and its small body.

Cavalier King Charles Spaniel came from the United Kingdom.

The average height of a Cavalier King Charles Spaniel is between twelve to thirteen inches.

Cavalier King Charles Spaniel are very intelligent dogs.

Cavalier King Charles Spaniel needs at least one hour of exercise daily.

Cavalier King Charles Spaniel has large eyes that are bright and round.

Cavalier King Charles Spaniel can enjoy sleeping under the covers with you.

The average litter size of a Cavalier King Charles Spaniel is five puppies.

Cavalier King Charles Spaniel has a feathery tail.

**Cavalier King Charles Spaniel
has a graceful walk.**

**Cavalier King Charles Spaniel
needs a jacket in the wintertime
for its daily walk.**

Cavalier King Charles Spaniel loves to cuddle with you.

Cavalier King Charles Spaniel enjoys sniffing in the outdoors, so keep on a leash.

The average weight of a
Cavalier King Charles Spaniel is
between eleven to eighteen
pounds.

Cavalier King Charles Spaniel
enjoys a set schedule.

Cavalier King Charles Spaniel
shed mostly in the spring and
fall.

Cavalier King Charles Spaniel is very adaptable to other animals.

Ronald and Nancy Reagan had a Cavalier King Charles Spaniel named Rex.

Cavalier King Charles Spaniel always looks happy to see you.

Cavalier King Charles Spaniel is not known to be a guard dog.

Cavalier King Charles Spaniel needs to be brushed at least three to four times a week.

For a toy dog breed, Cavalier King Charles Spaniel is one of the largest.

Cavalier King Charles Spaniel need their nails trimmed monthly.

Cavalier King Charles Spaniel can make a good therapy dog.

Cavalier King Charles Spaniel is still allowed in the House of Parliament in England.

Cavalier King Charles Spaniel makes an excellent companion dog.

Cavalier King Charles Spaniel is not an aggressive dog.

Cavalier King Charles Spaniel need interaction with their family.

Cavalier King Charles Spaniel is easy to be trained.

Cavalier King Charles Spaniel comes in four different colors;

King Charles is black and tan.

Prince Charles is black white, and tan.

Blenheim is a chestnut and white.

Ruby is mahogany.

Cavalier King Charles Spaniel always looks friendly.

Cavalier King Charles Spaniel would do living in a tiny home.

Cavalier King Charles Spaniel is
a toy breed, hot a hunting dog.

Cavalier King Charles Spaniel
enjoys mental stimulation.

Cavalier King Charles Spaniel fur is easily tangled on ears and legs.

When young, get your Cavalier King Charles Spaniel used to being groomed.

Find me on Amazon at:

Https://amzn.to/3oqoXoG

and on Facebooks at:

https://bit.ly/3ovFJ5V

Other Books by Michelle Hawkins

Series

Fun Facts on Birds for Kids.

Fun Fact on Fruits and Vegetables

Fun Facts on Small Animals

Fun Facts on Dogs for Kids.

Made in United States
Troutdale, OR
04/02/2024

18888246R00021